HOW YOUR BODY WORKS

Getting Energy

Pip Morgan

FRANKLIN WATTS
LONDON•SYDNEY

An Appleseed Editions book

First published in 2010 by Franklin Watts
338 Euston Road, London NW1 3BH

Franklin Watts Australia
Hachette Children's Books
Level 17/207 Kent St, Sydney, NSW 2000

© 2010 Appleseed Editions

Created by Appleseed Editions Ltd,
Well House, Friars Hill, Guestling,
East Sussex TN35 4ET

Designed by Helen James
Edited by Mary-Jane Wilkins
Artwork by Graham Rosewarne
Picture research by Su Alexander
Consultant: Steve Parker

ISBN 978 1 4451 0018 0

Dewey Classification 612.3'9

A CIP catalogue for this book is available from the British Library.

Photograph acknowledgements
page 4 A Inden/Corbis; 5 Awilli/Corbis; 6 Maximilian Stock Ltd/Science Photo Library; 7 Charles &
Josette Lenars/Corbis; 8 Jose Luis Pelaez/Blend Images/Corbis; 11 Eye of Science/Science Photo Library;
12 Steve Gschmeissner/Science Photo Library; 13 Biomedical Imaging Unit, Southampton General
Hospital/Science Photo Library; 15 Gastrolab/Science Photo Library; 16 Steve Gschmeissner/Science
Photo Library; 17 Saturn Stills/Science Photo Library; 21 Steve Gschmeissner/Science Photo Library;
23 (top) Thomas Deerinck,NCMIR/Science Photo Library, (bottom) Hybrid Medical Animation/Science
Photo Library; 24 Drew Kelly Photography/Corbis; 25 Larry Williams/Corbis; 26 Claus Lunau/Bonnier
Publications/Science Photo Library; 27 Science Photo Library; 28 A Crump, TDR,WHO/Science Photo
Library; 29 AJ Photo/HPR Bullion/Science Photo Library
Front cover Fred de Noyelle/Godong/Corbis

Printed in China

Franklin Watts is a division of Hachette Children's Books,
an Hachette UK company.
www.hachette.co.uk

Contents

What is energy for?

Your muscles need energy – without it they wouldn't be able to move, but your muscles are not the only part of your body that use energy. Every cell in your body needs energy to work well.

Giving you power

Your muscles use lots of energy to produce the power they need to contract or get shorter. When you concentrate on solving a problem the nerve cells in your brain use energy to power your thoughts.

Energy and power are essential for the cells in all your organs and tissues, including

The natural sugar in fruit such as apples help to provide energy.

your heart, kidneys, bones, liver and lungs, as well as your eyes, ears, teeth and skin.

Eating and breathing

Your body gets energy from the food you eat using oxygen from the air you breathe.

Getting energy involves chemicals that your body makes and your blood carries to your cells. The energy in your cells comes from burning fuel, although it doesn't burn in the same way as wood or coal, which make flames. The fuel your cells burn is a chemical called **glucose**. This is a simple sugar you get from digested food.

The oxygen you breathe is important, too. It needs to reach your cells at the same time as the glucose. Glucose and oxygen are carried around your body in your blood, but the real action takes place inside your cells. They release energy when they burn glucose with the help of oxygen.

Different chemicals

You are full of many different chemicals, which are called molecules. Molecules of water are the ones you have most of. You have probably heard of others, such as **carbohydrates**, **fats**, **proteins** and **vitamins**, because these are in your food.

Every time you do some exercise, such as skipping, you burn glucose to make energy.

BREAKING DOWN AND BUILDING UP

Every second your body is breaking down large **molecules**, such as carbohydrates, into smaller ones, such as glucose. It also combines smaller molecules to make bigger ones – for example to make proteins. The way your body breaks down some molecules and builds up others is called metabolism.

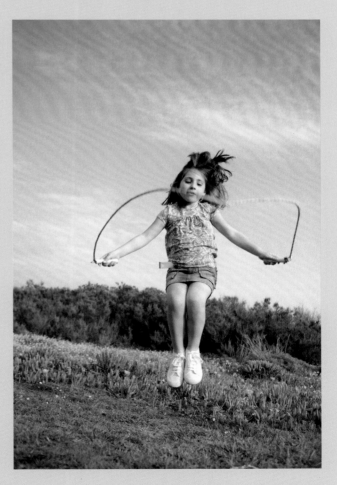

The fuel your body burns

Your body needs a supply of glucose and oxygen just to stay alive. Glucose comes from the food you eat and oxygen from the air you breathe. The oxygen allows your cells to burn glucose, which produces water and carbon dioxide – and releases energy.

Cereal grains, brown bread, pasta, potatoes and rice all contain complex carbohydrates.

Where does glucose come from?

Most of the glucose your body uses comes from the carbohydrates in the food you eat. Foods such as bread, rice and potatoes contain a complex carbohydrate called **starch**. Your **saliva** (see pages 10-11) and stomach break this down into glucose. Other foods, such as sugar and honey, also contain carbohydrates that your stomach can turn into glucose.

Your liver keeps a big store of glucose in its cells. It turns the glucose into a complex carbohydrate called **glycogen**. When your body needs a lot of glucose, the liver breaks down the glycogen into glucose and sends it round your body in your blood.

What else can you burn?

When you don't have enough glucose and your supply of glycogen is low, your cells may start to burn fats. Fats can give you more energy than glucose because fats contain more **kilojoules** – see pages 24-25.

TYPES OF SUGAR

There are all sorts of sugars in the food you eat. Table sugar, for example, contains **sucrose**. The sugar in fruit is called fructose and the sugar in milk is called **lactose**. Your body changes all these sugars to glucose and burns them to give you energy.

WHEN THINGS GO WRONG

Not enough food

People who are starving have burned all the fat in their bodies and then start to burn their protein. Burning protein gives you about the same amount of energy as burning carbohydrates. It is bad for your body because proteins form all the structures in your body, especially muscles. People with **malnutrition** (see page 28) do not have enough to eat. Their bodies have very little fat and so have to burn protein for energy.

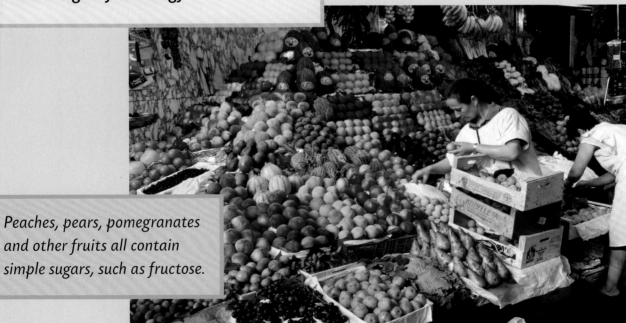

Peaches, pears, pomegranates and other fruits all contain simple sugars, such as fructose.

Feeling hungry

After you have eaten a meal you feel full. A lot of blood goes to your stomach and intestines as you digest and absorb the carbohydrates, fats and proteins that you have eaten. After a few hours of moving around and using energy you start to feel hungry again and then you want to eat more food.

Hunger pains

When you're hungry you get a feeling in your stomach known as pangs of hunger. This sensation of hunger starts after many hours without eating and is caused by your stomach muscles contracting quite strongly. Sometimes you feel so hungry it's almost painful. When you're very hungry all you want to do is find some food and eat it!

Eating a good meal with your family is better than snacking!

Did you know?
During your lifetime you will probably eat and digest about 30,000 kg of food. This is as much as six fully grown male elephants weigh!

Hunger starts when the brain tells the stomach to contract (pink arrow). Eating a meal puts food in your stomach which sends a message to the brain (green arrow) to turn off the hunger signal.

brain

message to turn off hunger signal

hunger signal

stomach

meal

In ancient times a Stone Age hunter had to go out and kill an animal for food before he and his family could eat. Today, many people in the world go hungry because they don't have enough to eat and cannot afford to buy food. You are probably lucky: all you have to do is go to the fridge and grab whatever you want!

What makes you hungry?
Many families eat breakfast, lunch and dinner at about the same time every day and one reason you feel pangs of hunger before a meal is that your body expects to eat. Another reason is that your stomach is empty. You also feel pangs when the amount of sugar in your blood falls below a certain level, which sends a signal to your brain that you need to eat (see above right).

An appetite
When you are expecting to eat, your mouth and stomach produce digestive juices that give you a pleasant feeling known as appetite. The smell and sight of food can also produce these juices.

Sometimes a person completely loses their appetite for food and can't eat anything. This may become a serious problem which can lead to an illness called **anorexia**.

Digesting food

Your body can digest almost any food – from hamburgers to raw fish to cabbage, ice cream and peanuts. Powerful chemicals in your **digestive system** break down the food into small particles and then your body absorbs as much as it can.

Mix and mash

Digestion starts in your mouth. When you chew your food, your teeth, tongue and jaws mix and mash it with your saliva. This liquid contains strong chemicals that start to break down carbohydrates called starches into smaller pieces.

When the food has become a gooey ball you swallow it in a gulp that pushes it down a tube called your **oesophagus** (say 'ee-sof-a-gus'). This tube has muscles which tighten and loosen in waves that push the ball of food into your stomach. From the moment you swallow, the food takes about six seconds to reach your stomach.

The food you eat starts its journey in your mouth, then travels down the oesophagus to your stomach. As it moves into your small intestine it mixes with juices from the pancreas and gall bladder.

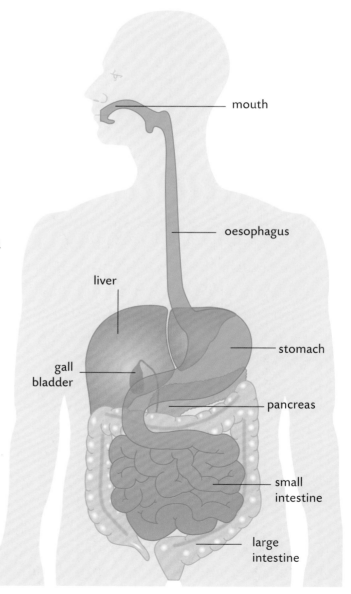

mouth

oesophagus

liver

gall bladder

stomach

pancreas

small intestine

large intestine

The lining of the stomach near the opening to the small intestine has many folds where a slimy liquid called mucus is made.

Inside your stomach

As you eat a meal, all the balls of food you swallow collect in your stomach, which grows bigger as more food arrives and it churns everything up. The stomach walls produce a powerful chemical to kill **bacteria** that enter with the food. Your stomach also makes a slimy liquid called **mucus** to protect the stomach walls from the powerful chemical.

Moving on

The churned-up food in your stomach is called **chyme**. After two to four hours the chyme starts to leave your stomach and goes into your small intestine. Here, the food is mixed with more juices that help to break the food down into simpler chemicals. Some of the juices come from the small intestine and others from an organ called the pancreas.

A yellowish-green liquid called **bile** also helps to break down the fatty substances in the chyme while it is in your small intestine. This bile comes from a small pouch called your **gall bladder**.

How your body absorbs food

As you digest the chyme, it passes along your small intestine, which has leaky walls to allow the goodness from the chyme to pass through them into your blood.

A huge area

The wall of your small intestine is not flat – it has millions of tiny finger-like folds called villi. Each of these has lots of smaller folds called microvilli. All these sticking-out pieces make a huge area which can absorb the chemicals, or nutrients, from the chyme into your blood. They also absorb quite a lot of water.

Your small intestine is about seven metres long, but the villi give it an area of about 250 square metres, which is about the size of a tennis court. Tiny blood vessels in the villi and microvilli absorb the nutrients from chyme and take them along a larger blood vessel to your liver. What's left of the food (about 400g every day) goes from the small intestine into the large intestine.

The lining of the small intestine has millions of deep folds called villi that absorb chemicals from the food (pink at top).

villus

small artery

small vein

lacteal

Each villus has its own blood supply and a vessel called a lacteal to collect fat.

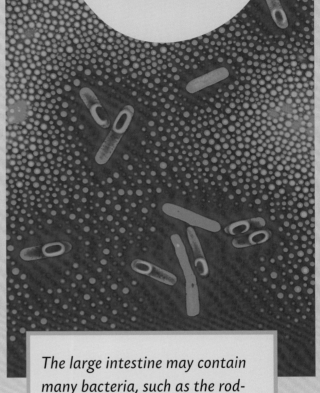

The large intestine may contain many bacteria, such as the rod-shaped bacteria known as E.coli.

Good bacteria

Various kinds of bacteria grow in the colon, which is the main part of the large intestine. We call them 'good' bacteria because they help your body make some vitamins, which are absorbed into your blood. The bacteria also defend your body against harmful organisms, although they die while they do this.

A SUGAR BOOST

When you eat a sugary snack, such as a chocolate bar, or drink something sugary, such as cola, your body quickly absorbs the sugars they contain. The level of glucose in your blood rises fast, giving you an energy boost. But the boost doesn't last long and, once it is used up, the amount of glucose in your blood falls quickly, leaving you with very little energy.

Getting rid of waste

What happens to the slushy, liquid chyme after the intestines have absorbed everything they can? It slowly moves through the large intestine and is turned into faeces (fee-sees). You push them out from your body when you go to the toilet.

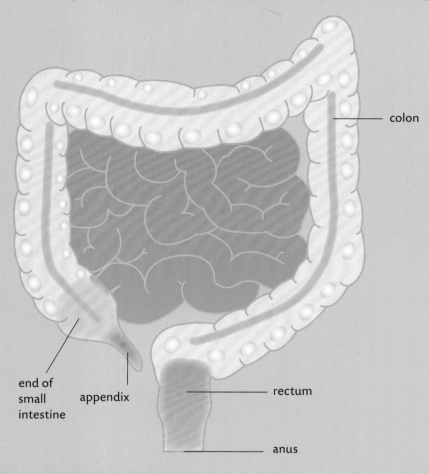

colon

The large intestine is a square shape. It is known as the colon, except for the appendix at the beginning and the rectum at the end.

end of small intestine

appendix

rectum

anus

Through the colon

Liquid food spends three to five hours in the small intestine then it goes into the first part of the large intestine. The main part of the large intestine is the colon. This is a muscular tube about 1.5 metres long. The lining of the colon absorbs salt and water from the liquid chyme, making it more solid, and turning it into faeces or poo. The lining also makes mucus to help faeces move along the tube.

Out the other end

The different muscles in the wall of the colon take it in turns to contract. These contractions churn up the faeces and

Did you know?

Your colon can absorb two litres of water every day.

The colon absorbs salt and water, then passes waste to the rectum.

move them along the tube. The faeces can spend anything from ten hours to several days in the long colon.

Two or three times a day, strong contractions push a large mass of faeces into the rectum, which is the last part of the large intestine. Here, the faeces are stored until you feel the urge to go to the toilet. Then muscles in the rectum and the anus below squeeze faeces from your body.

WHAT'S IN YOUR POO?

Faeces contains all sorts of things that your body can't absorb, such as fibre from the cell walls of the plants we eat. They also contain mucus and dead blood cells as well as the bodies of good bacteria.

YOUR APPENDIX

A small finger-like pouch hangs down at the start of your large intestine – this is your appendix. Humans don't use theirs, but animals do.

A cow uses its appendix to break down the food it eats, such as grass. If your appendix becomes swollen, perhaps as a result of an infection, you can get appendicitis.

Storing and using fuel

Your blood takes the glucose you absorb to your liver, where it is stored. It also carries glucose to the cells of your body, especially to your brain to keep you thinking. Every second, your brain checks the amount of glucose in your blood and makes sure your body has enough.

Liver store

Your liver is like a chemical factory in your body. Anything you don't need immediately is taken there and stored. Glucose, for example, is your body's fuel. But if there's too much in your blood then your liver removes it and stores it as a complex carbohydrate called glycogen. When your body needs more glucose, your liver releases some of its store into your bloodstream.

A capillary inside the liver contains many red blood cells.

WHEN THINGS GO WRONG

Diabetes

People who have a problem with producing or using insulin may have a condition called diabetes. They are diabetics and some of them need to take insulin regularly, usually by giving themselves an injection. They also need to be careful about what they eat and drink so they can control the level of glucose in their blood. If this level rises too high they may lose consciousness and slip into a **coma**.

A diabetic boy gives himself insulin using a pen-like device called a NovoPen.

Glucose control

The level of glucose in your blood is controlled by chemicals called **hormones**. Your pancreas produces a hormone called **insulin** and releases it into your bloodstream. If you have too much glucose in your blood, insulin helps your liver to store it. If your muscle cells need extra energy, then insulin helps them to take glucose from your blood.

When the cells of your body need to burn more glucose, two other hormones, called adrenaline and glucagon, are released into your bloodstream. Both of them help the liver break down some of its store of glycogen into glucose.

Did you know?

The liver is the only organ inside the body that can grow back, or regenerate itself. You only need about a quarter of a liver to grow a whole one – but it takes several years!

Oxygen for energy

Your cells need oxygen to help them burn glucose and release energy. Your lungs are perfectly designed to release oxygen into your blood. Breathing in and out is one of the most important things your body does, and it happens automatically.

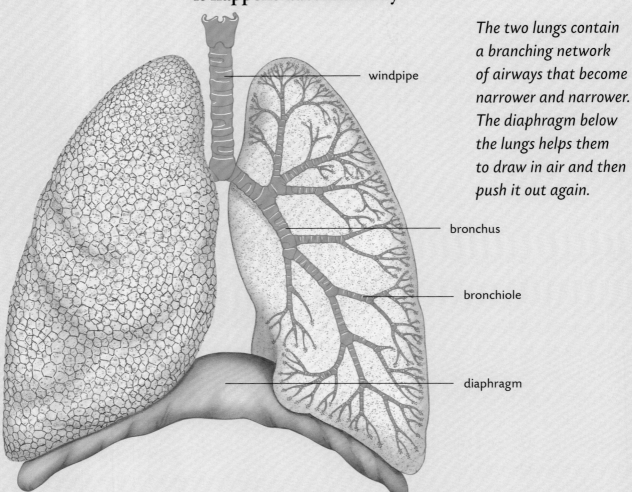

The two lungs contain a branching network of airways that become narrower and narrower. The diaphragm below the lungs helps them to draw in air and then push it out again.

windpipe

bronchus

bronchiole

diaphragm

How your lungs work

Your lungs are protected by your ribs, which form a kind of cage around them. Below the lungs is a very thick muscle called the **diaphragm** (di-er-fram). When your diaphragm and the muscles between your ribs contract, you breathe air in. When they relax, you breathe air out.

The movement of air

When you're sitting still, you breathe air in and out between 12 and 15 times

breathing in

breathing out

When you breathe in (far left) air fills your lungs as the diaphragm moves down. When the diaphragm moves up (near left) air leaves the lungs.

a minute. Every time you breathe in you take in about 500 ml of air. The air moves down your windpipe and into your lungs through two narrower tubes called **bronchi**. Each bronchus tube branches again and again into smaller and smaller tubes called **bronchioles**.

Eventually, the air finds its way to millions of tiny air sacs called **alveoli** (al-vee-oh-lee). These little sacs have very thin walls and are close to tiny blood vessels called **capillaries**. There are as many as 150 million alveoli in each lung.

Damp lining

Your breathing tubes are kept moist by a damp lining which has millions of tiny hairs called cilia (silly-a). These hairs move mucus up to the top of your lungs, along with any particles that you may have breathed in.

Did you know?
The network of air passages in your two lungs combined is about 2400 km long!

HEALTH CHECK
Measuring breathing

People who have problems breathing are regularly checked with a peak flow meter, particularly people who suffer from asthma. They take a deep breath, then breathe out as hard as they can into a wide tube. A pointer on the tube measures how much air they breathe out in litres per minute. People with asthma have narrow airways which means they breathe out less air than other people.

Swapping gases

Once you breathe oxygen into your lungs it needs to enter your blood, so it can be delivered to every cell in your body. At the same time, the carbon dioxide your cells dump in your blood goes back into your lungs to be breathed out.

Into the blood

The oxygen in the air you breathe in moves from your alveoli into the blood, which flows slowly through your capillaries (see page 22). There, the oxygen enters your red blood cells and sets off on its journey round your body. Carbon dioxide crosses in the opposite direction, from the capillaries and into the alveoli, where it turns into a gas and you breathe it out. This swapping, or exchange, of gases is part of a process called **respiration**.

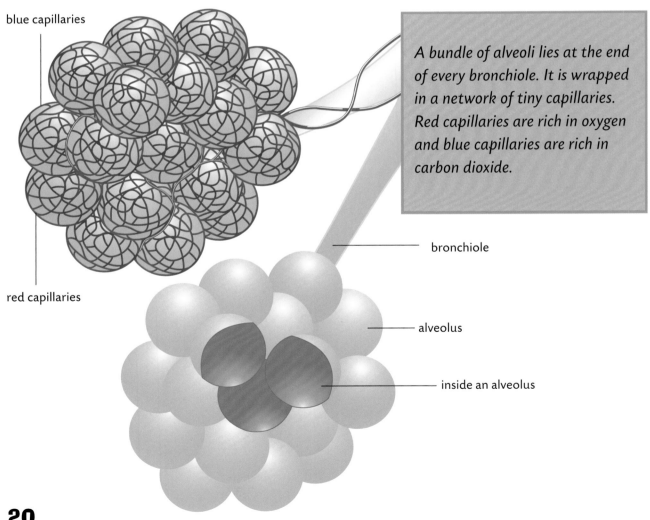

blue capillaries

A bundle of alveoli lies at the end of every bronchiole. It is wrapped in a network of tiny capillaries. Red capillaries are rich in oxygen and blue capillaries are rich in carbon dioxide.

red capillaries

bronchiole

alveolus

inside an alveolus

What's in the air?

The air you breathe into your lungs is mostly a gas called nitrogen. Your body doesn't need this gas, so you breathe it all out again. About a fifth of the air contains the oxygen your body needs. There is a small amount of carbon dioxide and tiny traces of other elements in air too.

A fair exchange

The way the gases move into and out of your blood is called **diffusion**. The air you breathe in contains more oxygen than the blood in your capillaries. Some of the oxygen diffuses, or drifts through, into your blood to make the balance equal.

At the same time, the blood arriving at the lungs has more carbon dioxide in it, so this gas passes out of your blood and into your alveoli. Then you breathe it out.

What makes you breathe?

You might think that you breathe in because you don't have enough oxygen in your blood. In fact the real reason is because there's too much carbon dioxide in your blood.

All the alveoli in your lungs are very close to thousands of red blood cells in the tiny capillaries.

SOAP IN THE LUNGS

The alveoli sacs in the lungs are very tiny – just 0.2 mm across – and they have very thin walls. They have to stay full so they can keep exchanging gases. To do this the lining of the sacs make a soapy substance, which stops them collapsing like empty balloons and filling up with fluid.

Making energy in your cells

Every cell in your body needs oxygen and glucose from
your blood. They find their way out of your blood
vessels and across each cell wall or **membrane**.
Once inside the cell, they are taken to special power
stations and used to make energy.

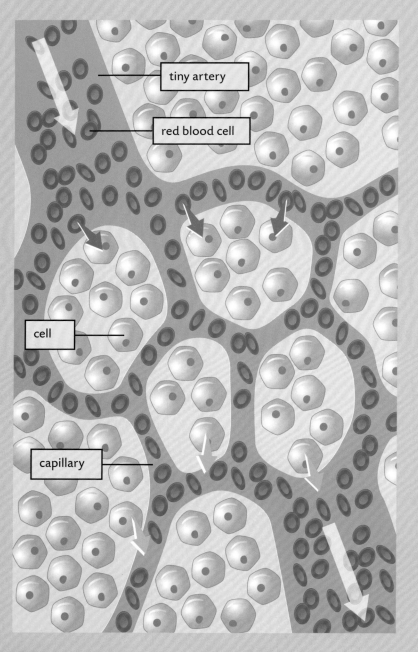

tiny artery

red blood cell

cell

capillary

Thin capillaries

The blood has to be very close
to the cells before it can release
its cargo of oxygen and glucose.
So your big blood vessels, called
arteries, branch into smaller and
smaller ones until their walls
are very thin. The tiniest blood
vessels with very thin walls are
called capillaries.

The blood flows through the
capillaries much more slowly
than through the arteries, so
there's plenty of time to transfer
the oxygen and the glucose.

*Blood flows through a tiny artery
(white arrow) and branches into
many capillaries. Red blood cells
deliver oxygen to the cells (red
arrows) while carbon dioxide
leaves the cells (green arrows)
and enters the bloodstream.*

A red blood cell (bright red) squeezes through a capillary (orange) as it delivers oxygen to the cells in heart muscle (green).

Coming and going

The membrane around a cell controls all the chemicals that enter and leave. Oxygen easily crosses the membrane, but glucose needs the help of a hormone called insulin, which is made in your pancreas and released into your blood. The insulin allows the glucose to travel through the cell membrane.

Power stations

Every cell has a nucleus and sausage-shaped structures where chemical reactions take place. They are called mitochondria (my-toe-kon-dree-ah). Here, the oxygen and glucose help to produce lots of chemical energy and some heat energy.

The cell either uses the chemical energy or stores it until it is needed, while the heat energy warms the cell. At the same time, the mitochondria make carbon dioxide and water as waste products.

The number of mitochondria in a cell depends on how much energy it needs. A liver cell may have 2000 because it needs to power lots of chemical reactions, but a skin cell may have less than 100.

A mitochondrion contains many folds where energy is made from glucose.

Your energy needs

Your body needs a certain amount of energy every day just to stay alive. Very active people need to make more energy than others. Energy comes from different types of food and we measure it in **kilojoules** (or kilocalories).

Who needs most energy?

We all need different amounts of energy. Children and teenagers need more kilojoules from their food than adults because they are growing and are usually very active. Older people need fewer kilojoules than younger adults because they are often less active. Pregnant women need many more kilojoules because they are feeding the baby growing inside them.

People who are very active use more energy than people who sit still for long periods of time. A footballer uses far more energy than someone watching football on TV. Some people use energy faster than others and so need more energy from their food.

How many kilojoules?

Scientists have calculated the number of kilojoules of energy we need to eat

Children and teenagers are very active and need lots of kilojoules to provide them with energy.

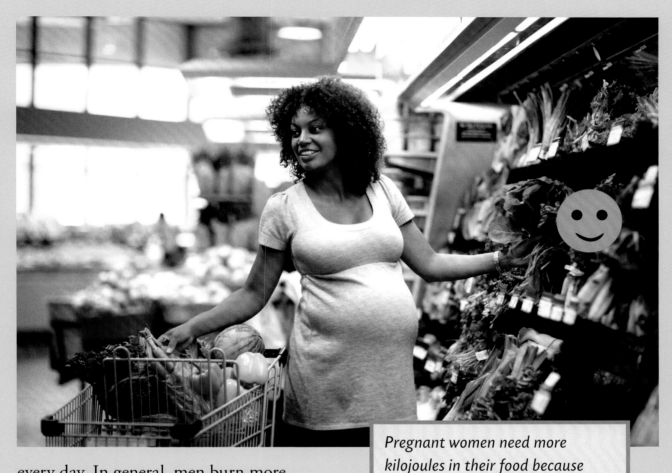

Pregnant women need more kilojoules in their food because they are eating for two people.

every day. In general, men burn more kilojoules than women, and babies and children need more as they grow bigger.

Babies aged up to five months need about 2730 kilojoules (kJ), which is about 650 kilocalories (kcal) a day. Toddlers aged one to three need to eat about 5460 kJ (1300 kcal) a day. Children between four and six need about 7560 kJ (1800 kcal).

Seven- to ten-year-olds need about 8400 kJ (2000 kcal) a day. Girls from 11 to 14 need around 9240 kJ (2200 kcal) a day, while boys the same age need about 10500 kJ (2500 kcal) a day.

Kilojoules from food

Foods contain different amounts of kilojoules. Vegetables have very few, but cooking oil and other fats contain lots. The amount of energy in a food depends on how much water it contains and whether it has lots of carbohydrates, fat or protein. These chemicals allow you to make different amounts of energy. One gram of carbohydrate or protein gives you 17 kilojoules, while one gram of fat gives you 38 kilojoules.

Body heat

Your body's cells produce heat energy all the time, particularly your muscle and liver cells. This heat helps to keep your body temperature normal at 37° Celsius.

Warm-blooded

Making energy produces heat in your body. The many chemical reactions that take place in your liver cells produce lots of heat. Every time your muscles contract they produce heat. The heat from your liver and muscle cells warms your blood as it passes through them.

If your temperature falls, your body burns more fuel and produces more energy to bring your temperature back to normal. Humans are warm-blooded animals because we can keep our body temperature steady. Other warm-blooded animals include gorillas, monkeys and chimps, as well as birds.

Muscle energy

Even when you are sitting down or standing still you are using your muscles. You use

37°C	37–36°C	36–32°C	32–28°C	28–25°C	below 25°C

A heat picture, called a thermogram, of two men. The man on the left is warm and has a normal body temperature of 37°C. The man on the right is very cold but his body still keeps his brain and his central organs at a normal temperature.

WHEN THINGS GO WRONG
Cramp

Have you ever had cramp? It can make a muscle feel like a painful knot. This can happen if you play a sport, such as football, for a long time. When the cells in your muscles run out of oxygen, they can still make energy and keep going for a short time, but they produce a chemical which collects in the muscle. This makes the muscle seem to seize up, which causes cramp.

Footballers often suffer cramp in the big calf muscles at the back of their legs. To relieve the cramp, they lie down with the leg in the air while someone stretches the muscle.

your diaphragm and rib muscles to breathe and the muscles of your skeleton to keep your body upright. When you exercise or play a sport, your muscles use a great deal more energy.

When you become very hot, your blood carries heat energy away from the places it is made to the surface of your skin, where it escapes from your body. This is why you look hot after exercise. Your skin also produces sweat, which helps to cool you.

Fight or flight

When you are in danger your body immediately prepares to react: you might fight the danger or run from it! When this happens, a chemical called adrenaline speeds up your breathing and heart rate and triggers the release of glucose fuel for your muscles to use.

Too little or too much food

Many people in the world don't have enough to eat and so suffer from malnutrition and starvation. At the same time, more and more people in developed countries, such as the US and UK, eat too much and are becoming fat, or even **obese**.

Not enough food

What happens to your body if you don't eat enough food to provide the energy and nutrients it needs? People who don't have enough to eat have little energy because their cells don't receive the glucose they need.

Instead, their bodies burn their stores of fat and their muscles. As a result, they grow thinner, lose weight and feel very tired. When all their fat has been burned, their bodies start to burn the protein in their cells – this is very dangerous and they may die.

People with malnutrition are not eating the proteins, fats, vitamins and minerals they need to lead healthy lives. This means they are more likely to catch infections because their bodies aren't strong enough to resist illness.

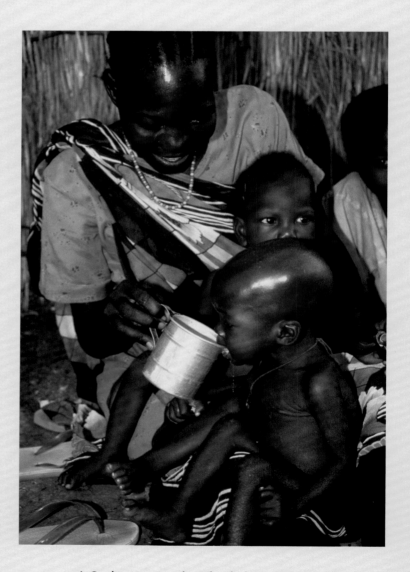

A Sudanese mother feeds her malnourished child with enriched milk.

Too much food

What happens to your body if you eat too many kilojoules? You put on weight. If you carry on eating too many kilojoules you may become fat and overweight. Very overweight people are called obese.

Some people put on weight more easily than others. How much you should weigh depends on how tall you are and how old you are. If you always eat more kilojoules than you burn, your body will turn the food into fat and store it in various parts of your body, increasing your weight.

The best way to lose weight is to exercise regularly and to cut down on foods that contain a lot of fat and sugar.

Teenagers who are overweight or obese take part in a special fitness class to help them lose weight.

PROBLEMS WITH DAIRY FOODS

Some people get stomach pains and diarrhoea when they drink milk or eat dairy foods (foods that contain milk). This is a problem with their digestive system which is called lactose intolerance – their system can't digest lactose, the natural sugar found in milk. These people have to avoid eating dairy products for the rest of their lives.

Glossary

alveoli   Tiny air sacs in the lungs where oxygen enters the blood and carbon dioxide leaves the blood.

anorexia   An illness in which a person stops eating because they are afraid of getting fat.

bacteria   A huge group of single-celled micro-organisms. Some types of bacteria cause serious diseases.

bile   A liquid that helps to break down fats.

bronchi   Airways that branch off the windpipe as it enters the lungs.

bronchioles   Airways that branch off the bronchi inside the lungs.

capillary   A tiny blood vessel that carries blood to the cells of the body.

carbohydrate   Chemicals that provide energy. Complex carbohydrates are an energy store and simple carbohydrates are burned to make energy.

chyme   Half-digested food produced in the stomach.

coma   When a person loses consciousness they slip into a coma.

diaphragm   The sheet-like, powerful muscle under the lungs that helps them breathe air in and out.

diffusion   The movement of a chemical from one place to another.

digestive system   The parts of the body, from the mouth to the large intestine, where food is broken down and absorbed into the blood.

fats   Greasy solids and liquids, such as margarines and oils, in food.

gall bladder   An organ near the liver that stores bile.

glucose   A simple sugar that the body's cells need for generating energy.

glycogen   A complex carbohydrate that is a store of glucose in the liver.

hormone   One of the chemicals that act as messengers in the body. Hormones help to control the way the body works and develops.

insulin   A hormone that helps glucose to enter cells and to be stored as glycogen in the liver.

kilojoule   A unit of energy contained in food.

lactose   A simple sugar found in milk and dairy products.

malnutrition   An illness caused by lack of food or eating an unhealthy diet.

membrane   A very thin layer which may be inside a cell, around a cell or a protective covering for a row of cells.

molecule A single unit or particle of certain chemicals.

mucus A liquid made by the body to stop membranes from drying out.

obesity A condition in which a person becomes very fat.

oesophagus Part of the digestive system which connects your mouth to your stomach.

proteins Chemicals that are essential for cells to grow and work.

respiration The process of breathing in oxygen and breathing out carbon dioxide.

saliva A fluid that stops the mouth from drying out and also helps to break down carbohydrates in food.

starch A complex carbohydrate in food such as potatoes.

sucrose A simple sugar in sugar cane.

vitamins Nutrients that are essential for health.

Books

Human Body Richard Walker, Dorling Kindersley 2004

The Oxford Children's A to Z of the Human Body Bridget and Neil Ardley, OUP 2003

Complete Book of the Human Body Anna Claybourne, Usborne Publishing 2006

Websites

www.biology4kids.com/files/cell_mito.html
Find out more about energy-producing mitochondria.

www.keepkidshealthy.com/index.html
Find out more about energy needs, diet and body weight.

www.biology4kids.com/files/systems_digestive.html
Find out more about how your digestive system works.

Index

MALPAS 7/7/18